THE SYSTEM

Keeping your Princess in Love
For Gentlemen only

Part 1

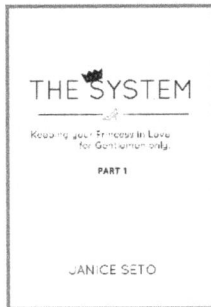

Janice Seto

The System: Keeping your Princess in Love, For Gentlemen Only

Cover designed by Janice Seto

This book is a work of fiction. Names, characters, places, and incidents either are products of the author's imagination or are used fictitiously. Any resemblance to actual persons, living or dead, events, or locales is entirely coincidental.

Visit my website at
https://www.janiceseto.com

Printed in the United States of America

Publisher: Janice Seto

ISBN-13: 978-1-926935-62-1 (ebook)
ISBN-13: 978-1-926935-60-7 (print)
ISBN-13: 978-1-926935-62-1 (audio)

CONTENTS

DEDICATION

1.What can Doc Love teach the royals?

2.Does a Gentleman propose to a woman he is not in love with?

3.Systems Guys do not waste her time

4.Do Gentlemen Marry women with whack-job Mothers?

5.What can go wrong if your kids don't like the woman you are dating?

6.Does the Confident Man insist his fiancée gives up her career?

7.My parents can't stand my married girlfriend

8.How does the Gentleman break up his sister-in-law's affair with a married man?

9.My girlfriend has too much good baggage

10. Why the rush? Patience is the key to women

11. A brother-in-law with convictions...

12. My fiancée's family's aren't our Big Fat Wedding... they gone nuts

13. My wife says I need a purpose...

14. She's wife material but not C-Suite wife material

The System For Her Series

ABOUT THE AUTHOR

ACKNOWLEGEMENTS

Mike

Paul

Bob

CHAPTER ONE

1.What can Doc Love teach the royals?

The Answer: Everything!

ON INDEPENDENCE DAY, DOC LOVE (www.doclove.com) and I met for lunch to celebrate the Fourth of July. Anytime you meet The Dating Dictionary guru, the man who has interviewed over 10,000 women, he who has received many a 'You Changed My Life' letter, it is an occasion for the memory book.

We talked about all sorts of topics – The System, his Mastery Series Challenge, The Truth Triangle, Cary Grant, and the 3 %ers. When the main course arrived, we got to the four-part series I had written, The System for Her: Doc Love Lessons in Betty Neels books.

I mentioned my first personality analysis book, Royalty Meets Enneagram, *Meghan Markle, Sarah Ferguson, Princess Tessy,* to which Doc Love responded, "They are clueless."

A man without The System, regardless if he is a prince at heart or a prince with a title, does not stand a chance.

Had any royal men put their egos aside and gotten The System or called for coaching, DocLove would have set them straight (Doc Love talks like this in person, not just on his radio show!) After all, Doc Love gets letters from all over the world, coaching men 'from Montana to Mongolia'. If he had received mail from men from the monarchies? The royals would be sleeping easier in the castle.

This book is set up as letters to Doc asking for his advice and the quick-witted responses that are Doc Love's take on relationships issues.

Doc Love's advice works for anyone, anywhere, any palace, any   place.

CHAPTER TWO

2. Does a Gentleman propose to a woman he is not in love with?

Hello, Doc,

I heard about you from a cousin and read a couple of your articles online so I am contacting you about a situation I find myself in. I am heir to the fortunes of an internationally well-known family (think Kennedy + European royal) and my family is now pressuring me to get married to anyone suitable and sire children of my own.

Not that I crave the rug rats as I like my bachelor life just the way it is right now. I get plenty of attention from Caprices wherever I go. Truth be told, my face is rather unique so I know it is actually due to my family

money and social cachet that I can pull in the truly beautiful types who want to have babies with me (and the foxy married types who want to have fun with me).

If I fail to leave offspring, then my brother, the next-in-line, will become increasingly important as my official heir. That means I would have to spend more time with him in the future than I already do. Which would be unbearable as the Good-Looking-One-of-the-Family is not the sharpest pencil in the box. I am about a couple decades his senior and we had never spent much time together. Frankly, we don't have much in common.

A few years ago, I made it known I would get married around age 30. Does time fly when you are having fun! Now I am a couple years past the Big 3-0 and I boxed myself in.

Papa's great uncle died last year and I was griefstricken by the loss of this family patriarch. It was tough to look stoic during the public funeral and only one person sympathized with me. She is just about 20 and works in a daycare. Even though she has money of her own, she prefers to have four other girlfriends share her apartment. London is the place to be these days!

Her family and mine have known each other for centuries. It is a good match, and everyone in my family likes her. My father and others of that generation advised me to propose to her, as she is a rare catch and young enough to learn how to carry out our charitable duties and on the social rounds. They also said if I am not serious about marrying her, then let her go before the media ruin her life.

So, Doc, what should I do? She is a nice girl and is very suitable. I am thinking I should give it a go, and if it doesn't work out with her, then I can do whatever I want as long as I am discreet. I could see my girlfriend on the side. (I can't marry Caprice as she already is married with children.)

Signed, Alex, sad to Settle for 'Suitable'

Hello, Alex, sad to Settle for 'Suitable'

You have come to the right place. My name says it all, I am a Love Doctor. For Men. That's my speciality, not family dynamics therapist or marriage counsellor. Because when you get married, it is between you and her. Not family and you and her. Don't listen to those blood relatives – marriage is forever.

Deciding what kind of woman is 'suitable' for you is solely up to YOU. The System is designed to make Gentlemen out of men, and Gentlemen think for themselves. As my cousin Fast Eddie Love in East LA says, "Once I turned 15, I told Ma, 'I pick my own clothes now.' "

About children, you really do like the cutie-pies, don't you? Now, 'do you want them?' is not the right question. What you want to know is 'do you want children now?' If now is not the time because you are having the time of your life, then you got nothing to explain to nobody. The more money you have, the handsomer you are to all women! Even the married ones. To those with wedding rings on, just give them a smile and say, "You got any single girlfriends you can introduce me to?"

All this talk about your Gaspard Ulliel look-a-like brother is a distraction. A good-looking guy without The System is a clueless good-looking guy.

Ultimatums don't work, Grasshopper, the ones they put on you and the ones you put on yourself. You need to get out of the box and keep your trap shut about your private life. Gentlemen are not exhibitionists! Nor are they wimps for the family. Explain it away with a Confident shrug, "Was I ever young when I said that! Nowadays, I let God figure out when to bring me Ms Right."

Sorry about losing the family patriarch and bravo at the service. That is what a Spartan does, honoring the Big Man at his funeral and letting the focus be on HIS life, not you. Of course you felt strong emotions, we are not robots!

So, Alex, this teenager comes to you with her condolences - I have faith in humanity! Daycare teachers do that day in and day out, to everyone. Not saying that you aren't special but think about it: every morning in class, guaranteed, some kid is going to stub his toe or cry over the hamster and she has to comfort the weeping child or the entire brood will join in with the tears. Sympathy for anyone feeling sad comes with the daycare job. Her commiserating with you is something she does for everyone. This may be hard for you to hear and I don't want to run the bus over you but I have to repeat: you probably ain't that special to her.

She makes a living looking after kids and I go one step further, she seems good looking after her money. When she has friends staying over and go about collecting rent from her friends, this is a landlord we are talking about, Alex! But until you get 10 to 15 dates in with her, and she has no Red Flags, and you raise

Interest Level, nothing counts. Not even that she does landlady on the side.

It is a nice factoid that your families have known each other since Henry VIII was roaming around merrie ole England with one of his six wives. But let's not forget that the only number that counts is 20. The daycare teacher is not even 20. She's too young! Remember in the Dating Dictionary - which you should order for immediate download and read 15 times - until she gets to age 23, she is a ding dong, falling in love and falling out of love every 5 minutes.

For me, what removes her from the Suitable category is your entire attitude towards her. You are not in love with her! All your talk is about her fit and her learning and other mumble-jumble. I am a Love Doctor and the biggest obstacle is you have 49% Interest Level in her, and dropping.

When Interest Level is below 50%, there is nothing to work with. Your heart is not in marrying her, so quit being a guy with no backbone and stand up for yourself and stand up to your family. Be a Gentlemen and let her go with a clean break.

Otherwise, you would be proposing to a teenager who has stars in her eyes and romance with a capital R in her heart. Otherwise, your new wife will get the rude awakening that you have a married girlfriend in the background – the one you actually call Caprice! (C'mon, Alex, I know you are not a System guy when you go for the ones who already have another man's ring on her finger.) Then the wife you do not love will have every reason to be mad at you. She will feel used and will whip up a fresh dish of wifely hell every day of your married life.

Remember, guys, if you marry her because of family pressure, your bride's husband is a Wimpus Americanus.

CHAPTER THREE

3.Systems Guys do not waste her time

Hello, Doc,

A friend of mine told me to write in with you on my dilemma. I am a 32 year old executive living in New York who travels to the West Coast a lot in my job. Yesterday, I had been given an ultimatum by a girl I have been dating for 10 years: marry me or get lost. This English girl is not the love of my life so there is no way I am giving in.

I have been back in the States for a couple years now after almost a decade in London. My father still works all over the world in his consulting business and he and my mother had made England their European base for a while. It was convenient for me to do a study-abroad in the UK. Her cousin was a college chum of mine and introduced me to her. She was 19 and I was 21 at the time.

You know how the British class system is over there if you watch shows like Downton Abbey. She and her cousin are at the top of that food chain, which helped me socially. It was a five-star lifestyle! We were invited to premieres, launches, celebrity events, and I gave the media my best profile. I still get residual attention now because of it.

Now, I have to say that I worked hard as well as played hard. I climbed the corporate ladder in London. Eventually, I became an executive with a very well-known US tech company and came home. A few months later, she decided to get work in the US too and got a job that gives her all the time she wants to fly back and forth to London.

Her family would like us to get married because we had a decade together but I am not going to let anyone steamroll me into that. I do not want to marry her, period. The UK is not where I want to live, especially with Brexit. That lifestyle is not for me anymore. Besides, I don't need to do long distance because here in New York, I can get a date in a second.

I am going to cut her loose. So, Doc, how do I break up with her without looking like a cad?

Bruno, the Getting Out Guy

<u>Hi, Bruno, AKA Getting Out</u>,

Young, that's what you are, you are never old, so you are 32 years young. You are smart in your choice of friends. You fill him in on your dilemma and he gives you good advice. Now I am reading your letter: here's what I say.

After you read my reply, you order The Dating Dictionary ASAP so you don't lose another decade of your life. As my cousin, General Love, would say, "Your looks are your ammo and, at age 40, your ammo's mostly gone."

I highly approve of studying. And when you study in a different country, you soak up the culture and meet people. You make connections and take networking to a whole different level. It's a tough world out there and you leveraged it to a corner office. That's beautiful.

What I do not recommend is dating when you are temporary. That was your first mistake. It does not matter if it is 7 months or 7 years that you are out of the country, you intend to come home! So, Bruno, this was dead-in-the-water from the get-go. Unless you move and get citizenship over there or she comes over and takes out a Green Card, you are spinning your wheels.

Another reason this was a no-go from the get-go: She was 19 and you were 21 and you were her walker and she was your arm candy. I get it. Do you now get that you were both young dingdongs who were mutually getting something out of it? You got entry to the fantasyland of the English upper class and she got a good-looking guy her dingdong friends could envy her for. It is not using someone when there is mutual benefit, Dog.

Your mistake is you were too young to get exclusive. And you were playing in the twilight zone sandbox of exclusive at least six years too long. As the System says, before the age of 23, you are both ding dongs. When she turned 23, you should have either married her or dropped her. That's what a Gentleman does but you are forgiven (by me) as you were not trained in The System then.

When you had sinking Interest Level or when you planned your move Stateside, you should have sat her down before you hopped on the plane and said, "When I went over for the job interview, I met someone and I fell in love with her. I'm sorry. You are a great person and I wish you the best." And then after a couple minutes of taking your lumps, you beat it out of there.

It is not too late to do it now, that's the System's response to her ultimatum.

There is no way to avoid looking like a cad. You wasted ten years of her life. Worse, you wasted 10 years of your own life! But at least you can blame it on youth.

The best thing you can do is show everyone you won't cave in and do something egotistical like get engaged when you don't love the girl. Marriage is enough hard these days and when the groom is the one who has less than 49% Interest Level, her family might as well have a divorce lawyer lined up.

That's what a Confident man does, stay true to what is good for him. But you won't stay Confident until you do the right thing early. When she proves not to be the Caprice for you, the Confident man gets rid of her the very second you know. Then when you do get a good girl, the only way to keep Caprice in love with you is you buy The Dating Dictionary and live and breathe the System.

Remember, guys, a Gentleman does not waste time, hers or his.

CHAPTER FOUR

4. Do Gentlemen marry women with whack-job Mothers?

Hello, Doc,

I have been dating a very nice Caprice. She is a hard worker, positive, volunteers with charities, and always up for a social gathering with family and friends. Plus, she loves me! I love her too. She has no Red Flags, Doc, so why am I hesitating to pop the question after 2 years. Three words: her whack-job mother.

Her Mother is the life of the party. She lives for the limelight and serves the best food at no expense spared. She is no longer an A-lister after divorcing Caprice`s father but still gets invited to all the celebrity events because Mother is witty and always game for the photographers. Unfortunately, she is terrible with money and has been bankrupt twice. The cash setback doesn`t really stop her love of the high life.

Caprice and her sister are in their late twenties and have grown up with their mother saying something tacky ending up on the media or dressing too tight and too young or getting attention for some get-rich-quick scheme about every few months. She has been on reality shows too. Her love life used to make headlines (that broke up her marriage) but that has stopped since Mother has aged out. To be frank, she no longer has the pull on men like she used to.

The sisters just keep their heads down and work. They don't want to be their mother`s sounding board but Mom just ploughs in and spills out everything from the highs of the party to the lows of credit card arrears.

It also got to the point where they felt it was their job to rescue their mother from her debt collectors. Their father, who has the money, put a stop to it before the emotional extortion got really started. A few years ago, he simply moved her into his house just so the girls know their mother has a home.

Mother sounds a bit irresponsible and she is. I am afraid what will happen when their father dies and then Mother would look to my wife (I would really love to marry her) and her sister for support. Caprice and I work hard for our money and I had no hesitation in telling Mother that our wallets are closed to her and to get a real job. This was even before Caprice's father stepped in. Any advice?

Carlo, who is the Hiding My Wallet Guy

<u>Hi, Carlo,</u>

Caprice and you sound like a couple of love birds. You both work and you are at the right age. You sound like you are taking it slow and have the same goals. But remember, without the System, you won't keep her in love with you so I advise you to invest the $99 bucks.

Mother is not a keeper, not honest with reality, no loyalty to her husband, can't trust her with money, looking in my dictionary, she is a real Party Girl. An over-the-hill Party Girl who loves the camera.

To pay the bills, Mother asks her daughters and their boyfriends to open up their bank accounts... Am I hearing this correctly? The woman has no shame. And she would be the grandmother of your children...! As my cousin Fast Eddie Love from East LA says, "What a sign of good breeding...!"

But this really is not your problem, Carlo. As my cousin, Reverend Love says, "Give to Caesar what is Caesar's and give to God what is God's." In other words, let her mind her own business and you take care of your own.

If you marry Caprice, she alone has to stop the Whack–Job Mom problem from leaking onto her. What you have to do is check carefully that she is able to do so and is willing to do that. She might not want to do put up the boundaries and THAT, my friend, would a Red Flag. A daughter who won't say, "That's not my problem, Mom, look elsewhere for your solution," might be the sign of someone who can't stand up for herself in other areas. You need The System.

It is irritating when the same problems come up over and over again with some people, but the System protects you. (Without it, you could have dated a version of the flakey Mother and not the hardworking daughter. Look at your future father-in-law to see how that turned out.) Having said that, Caprice should verify what her Father has put into place financial-wise for his ex-wife in his will. That would be the best parting gift for his children.

Remember, guys, if she can't handle her whack-job mother while you two are dating, she can't handle mom after the wedding.

,

Chapter Five

5.What can go wrong if your kids don't like the woman you are dating?

Hello, Doc,

My wife and I are very happy together. After so many years in love, since we were in our early twenties and during our first marriages and 2 children each, we decided not to waste any more time apart and I asked her to move in with me. Now, four years onward, we finally got permission to marry and I so look forward to coming home after a hard day of work. Domestic bliss for us two middle-aged people.

My family is very prominent and has been so for many generations. We each have a comfortable trust-fund income source which makes life go along rather pleasantly. The only fly in the ointment are my two adult sons, now in college. **They have a rather poor attitude towards their new stepmother.**

It is rather embarrassing as her own side has been splendid. Her own two children have married and have their own lives and have accepted me as their mother's second husband. Even her first husband has been civil – he had messed around first in their marriage, and has since remarried.

My sons have this attitude that my second wife is taking their late mother's place. This is nonsense as I had told them that my late ex-wife never ever had a place in my heart. It is illogical to even think that my second wife, the love of my life, would be stepping into my ex-wife's footsteps.

Their froideur started the first vacation from boarding school after my darling moved in. She has always been kind to them when they came home on holidays but they responded either by ignoring her or surreptitiously countering her directions to the household staff. It has gotten to the point that my darling was made to feel unwelcome in her new home by their passive-aggressive behaviour.

So, Doc, what should I do about my sons? I won't let them disturb my happy domestic life.

Daniel, who wants a Smooth Blend

Hi, Daniel,

Let me get this right, you moved your girlfriend into the family home, while your sons were at boarding school, and this is the woman whom you committed adultery with while their mother was still alive. And you honestly thought they would roll out the welcome mat? They are very faithful to their mother's memory. As my cousin, Reverend Love, would say, "Boys are devoted to their mother because she is the first woman who loved them!"

Of course those sons are acting passive-aggressive. Because if they were full-on aggressive, they know you would stop their allowances. As my cousin, Fast Eddy Love from East LA, says, "They know which side their Whole Foods bread is buttered!"

In case you think your personality is the reason her children like you, I quote two words you wrote: Trust Fund. It must BE large enough that even her ex-husband thinks you are a stand up guy. That is a good use of money, buying domestic peace from the blended characters in this marital drama.

One thing going for you is your honesty. But spraying honesty all over the place serves you no good. Because your indiscriminate honesty comes from a husbandly defend-her-reputation reflex caused by your extremely high Interest Level in your second wife. Daniel, you have to filter like a good barista at Starbucks. You have to rein in your Interest Level because it is getting in the way of your parenting role.

Another thing – you are all worked up about the wrong thing. You are all concerned that your second wife feels unwelcome in her new home. How about your own sons feel unwelcome in their family home?

Telling your sons you never loved your mother is a big slap in the face. Go make an appointment with the private wealth guy at your bank – get ready to pay some expensive shrink with a real sheepskin to fix the blow to their self-esteem. What do I tell you – no negatives, no put downs, no heavy subjects, because it does not raise Interest Level nor does it raise Respect. Yes, Guy, you were disrespectful to their mother. Mom, especially a late lamented Mom, in case you don't know, is off-limits.

Your only comment about their mother going forward is 'Your Mother was a fine woman who loved you very much. We tried our best but we could not make it work out.' That's all you say. You don't speak ill of the dead when it comes to their dead mother.

I used to live in Los Angeles AKA La-La-Land and then I relocated south to San Diego years ago but it looks like you moved right on in! I know you want a smoothly blended family but it ain't going to happen. It is all set up wrong from the get-go decades ago so, at best, you get people going through the motions.

When your boys plan to be home, your honey has just got to get outta town and I suggest you book a long cruise of the Black Sea or the Hawaiian Islands, Hey, you can afford it, and she will love not being in Awkward Land. Your sons will spend quality time with the only parent they have left. You can do it and you should do it, guy.

What you can also do is do the math - sooner or later, the sons will finish their college and get lives and apartments of their own. Isn't that what trust funds are there for? I give it ten years max for you to fork over the dough for her cruise vacations.

Remember, guys, when you love her, make sure your Interest Level won't cause others to detest her.

CHAPTER SIX

6.Does the Confident Man insist his fiancée gives up her career?

"Hello, Doc,

I have come across your columns online just recently. Last week I ordered The Dating Dictionary and been reading as much as I can. As a 32 year old very eligible bachelor working in the family firm in my country's capital, I should have a lot of luck with the ladies. But I do not and your Dating Dictionary is a big help.

Last month, I met Caprice at a reception. Somehow the family subtly arranged for all sorts of eligible women to be there and I had a whale of a time. Most of them were pretty but it was the Caprice with the added dollop of smarts that I found most compelling. We had a great conversation about studying abroad, learning foreign languages, and working in high-octane environments. Since that first meeting, I have met her for afternoon tea a few times since then.

She is my dream girl, nice looks, brains, and the drive to use it. I would love to marry her. But here is my concern. Anyone who marries me marries my family. Everyone here knows our reputation of being ultra conservative. The men go out in the world and work and the women stay busy with children, charitable works, and social functions. You know the mother in Crazy Rich Asians? Imagine her but with a royal title, that is my Mom.

Caprice would have to conform to the ceremonial role of being my wife. That means anyone who marries me is full-time at home. The career wife thing is just not done in my family.

I know Caprice's Interest Level in me is sky-high as it was she who brought up the subject of marriage. It was a heart-to-heart conversation, I could hear her angst as she shared how important her career is. She had gone overseas to study at an Ivy League and has her eye on an executive career or an ambassadorship.

A traditional marriage and being a conventional wife is something she just does not want.

So, Doc, what should I do? She is smart and ambitious and I am wildly in love with her but the role of my wife is set in stone.

Ernest, the Must Cha-chan-change her Guy

<u>Hello, Ernest,</u>

Thanks for taking your future seriously enough to take action and buy The Dating Dictionary. More men should just get off the fence and put their egos aside. My System will change you and that leads to a change on how women look at you, even if you weren't loaded with good (family) fortune.

I am not going to rag on you since you just got The Dating Dictionary and have not yet read it 15 times. But go back and look at my writings on Interest Level. It is HER Interest Level in you that matters with Caprice, not yours in hers. She is pretty and has brains, she has had men in love with her since high school, and you just joined the crowd.

When a Caprice has high IQ when you met her, that's something she gets to keep. No one can change that, not even you. As my cousin Rabbi Love says, "My son, God passed out to her a large helping of brains."

How do I know that? Because of how you got played into thinking she was serious about marriage to you the minute she brought up the M word.

Here's what really happened, Ernest. The brainiac that she is did not accidentally bring up the subject of marriage under the pretext she wanted you as her husband. Your high Interest Level in her gave you false hope that she wanted to marry you and have your babies and that's why she is talking wedding rings.

In reality (and you will get to the Reality Factor in my book soon) is she had to pop your euphoric In-Love bubble ASAP before you got really down the Road-of-Love, to let you down gently, and to do it so that you don't feel rejected as men can't deal with rejection. She deployed the age-old tactic, the pre-emptive dump.

When you harped on your family's traditional expectations, whatever Interest Level she had in you sunk like an anchor. What do I say when you first meet Caprice, No negatives, no heavy subjects! But to your credit, you laid your cards on the table like the honest guy you are.

While I am on this track, do not blame her low Interest Level on your conservative family. You are very conservative too! And she didn't like that confirmation of career-free future with a royally nagging mother-in-law.

By letting you raise all the reasons that Caprice's career is not suitable to married life with you, she primed you to verbalized all the obstacles you would encounter with her as a prospective bride.

Hey, I gotta hand it to this Clever Caprice: Mission accomplished, that's why you are writing to me. Face the facts, guy, the cards (Red Flags!) are stacked against you and your relatives welcoming her and her briefcase into the family compound. By playing it this way, she has given you permission to use the Rejection card on her.

In life, we rarely get dealt a good hand. Well, guy, go use that Rejection card and say 'Sayonara, sweetheart!'

Since it is so obvious that she won't change her career plans and you won't change what you need in a wife, ther. you have to look elsewhere. Don't worry about hurting her feelings - Caprice never had more than 55% Interest Leve. in you anyways. That's the other thing, her Interest Leve.

in her career (95%) is higher than her Interest Level in you (55%).

Go look for what you need and don't look back. You didn't know her well, and what you did find out wasn't to your liking, and you will soon fall for someone else. The magic word is "Next!"

Remember, guys, the smart girl would never give up her IQ in order to marry you, so move on. As my cousin Fast Eddy Love in East LA says, "Airheads need love too."

CHAPTER SEVEN

7.My parents can't stand my married girlfriend

Hello, Doc,

I need help with my family, who are shunning my girlfriend. A couple buddies of mine shared your site and, from the articles I binged on, you seem to have all the answers.

Last spring, I first met Caprice at a charity function I was hosting at my weekend country house. It had been another long week at the family business when I drove down after lunch on Thursday. The job is weighing me down, but as the first-born son, it is my responsibility to my father and mother to work there along with my siblings. But I had bargained with them to have weekends off, so I usually take off on Thursday afternoon and return mid-morning Monday. Blowing off steam is the only way I can cope with the drudgery of toeing the line. My father is an arch conservative who does not move with the times. I have stopped putting forth ideas to him and basically just give him lip service.

So after a work week of restraint, I was ready for some female companionship, and wow, Caprice, I have never been so fascinated with a woman. She is so refreshing, is not sucking up to me, and is witty. She tells it like it is while others are yes-men or yes-women.

There were five other couples staying as guests and we were so relaxed. I invited this merry crowd back often for weekend breaks. I am not sure when I fell for her, but I did know by Christmas, she was the only woman I wanted to be with. Caprice is so authentic, she even tells me off – I love it when she busts my chops and treats me like a real human being.

I dropped all my other girlfriends like a hot potato and Caprice is gradually getting exclusive too. She is still living with her husband until I can convince her to marry me. But that does not interfere with my helping her out with her personal expenses. I have introduced her to haute couture and she looks like a million bucks now that there is real jewelry as well. Not only does she look like she belongs to my social set, they have all taken her into their bosom.

All except my fuddy-duddy parents. They refuse to invite her over and say she is not suitable. I think if they got to know her, they would love her. But because they are adamant, the only times I could have them meet her are public functions where I make sure we all cross paths.

On the other hand, the younger generation, including my siblings are supportive, they say 'as long as she makes you happy'.

I am starting to get really ticked off that the parents and aunts and uncles are united against my Caprice. If they do not roll out the welcome mat for her, I am seriously contemplating chucking the whole business and securing a big severance package. That way we can set up house and that would show them how good a match we are.

So, Doc, where do I go from here?

Felix, the Stand By Your Gal Guy

Hello, Felix, The Stand By Guy,

I don't believe in dating-by-committee and I think dating-with-parental-approval a load of hogwash. You did not choose your parents but they get to choose your spouse, where's the logic in that? In a happy marriage, the key ingredients are two people who have high Interest Level in each other and the Truth Triangle.

What's that, you say? Go online to www.doclove.com and you can order The Dating Dictionary, to start learning The System. You can binge-read my online articles all you can but that's the tip of the iceberg. Do yourself a favour and buy The Dating Dictionary, instead of expensive baubles for your girlfriend.

You would learn how important is Interest Level. And the Interest Level of Caprice in YOU. In your letter, I can tell your Interest Level in her is in the stratosphere. But as for her Interest Level in you, I have to break it to you, guy, it obeys the law of gravity.

Here's another essential element of The System my columns mention that you obviously misinterpreted – when I say no ex-boyfriends and ex-husbands lurking in the background, I don't mean current husbands in the foreground is acceptable!

What you don't get is that you are a Stand By. Here in SoCal, we have all sorts of dinner theater and soap operas. When the lead actor or actress is off sick, the Stand By jumps into the role. Later on, when the lead actor returns to the set or stage, the Stand By is yanked back into the shadows. She has more Interest Level in her husband than you – how do I know that? Her toothbrush is at his place. And she has two turkeys on her string – how do I know that? He hasn't kicked her toothbrush out of his place. Some women are like that, your Caprice must be insecure enough to need men dangling, the more desperate the men, the merrier.

Do you know why your family can't stand your married girlfriend? Because they care about you.

I don't like it when guys help married women break their vows, even though in this case, it sounds like she has tapdanced on hers a long time ago. You wouldn't like it if some man fooled around on your girlfriend on you. And you wouldn't like it if your wife fooled around in front of you. Your only luck is that her husband has not come at you with a baseball bat... yet.

As for loyalty, Felix, let me ask you a question: What makes you think Caprice would be more loyal to you than she is with him? She's wired for playing the field. You are lucky that her husband is not wired for greet you with a shotgun. But maybe you like being submissive to her controlling nature. When she busts your chops, and you like it, that is dominatrix and submissive dynamic. (Look that up sometime.) Whatever happens, the ball's in her court because you and her husband are begging for her attention and accept whatever scraps she throws at you. You are the antithesis of Challenge.

Enough about Caprice, the least loyal wife I have come across this decade. Now, guy, I have been doing this for over 30 years and I have a good nose for what's off. Maybe you aren't aware of it so let me shine a big spotlight what's off about your situation. If you don't want to work in the family business for whatever reason like your Dad is a macho boy or it ain't a good fit, then hand in your notice, negotiate yourself a severance package, and vacate the corner office.

Sure, you will sacrifice some of your cushy lifestyle but as my cousin Fast Eddy Love in East LA says, "H. Stern called to say they are closing your account, guy, you can't have it both ways!"

What a Gentleman does not do is make his quitting look like it was due to his girlfriend's unsuitability. That is disrespectful to her. When you make a clean break with the business, do not pass the buck on your decision. Only a

Wimpus Americanus throws his girlfriend under the bus. The Confident Man takes his medicine like a man and tells the parents 'I am not interested in doing this anymore.' Leave her out of it.

Remember, guys, if you are no longer in love with your spouse, you divorce them, you don't date around them. When you can't stand your job, just quit without dragging your girlfriend into it.

CHAPTER EIGHT

8.How does the Gentleman break up his sister-in-law's affair with a married man?

Hello, Doc,

Help prevent me from beating up my sister-in-law's secret boyfriend and going to jail!

My wife and I have been busy the past few years since we got married and started a family. We both work part time for the family business too. Just over Christmas, We just stumbled upon the fact my 20 year old SIL is secretly carrying on with one of my Father-in-Law's executive assistants. Not only is he breaking the Human Resources policy against dating, the 'fishing off the company pier' , the bastard is 15 years older than her and married with 2 young toddlers. She is not working, living at home, occasionally puts on an appearance at company events, and should be having the time of her life with available bachelors.

It hasn't become a full-blown affair yet but even an emotional affair is dangerous. My Father-in-law has had serious health issues for about 4 years and my Mother-in-Law is preoccupied with him. They think she has a normal innocent fleeting crush but have no idea the bastard is encouraging her. Worse, the bastard is a trusted advisor who mixes with them socially.

I'm not saying he is waiting for my FIL to die so he can divorce his wife and marry my SIL and be set for life but the family corporation is doing very very well...

His current job comes with a good salary and house, which would all disappear if my FIL finds out and loses his famous temper. My naive SIL would have her silly dreamworld come to an abrupt end and my wife is worried about her being hurt. My wife does not like conflict and prefers to stay out of it. Better that than SIL wasting her time is my opinion.

So Doc, should I take him aside and tell him to get out of town? Or should I tell my Father-in-Law?

Gustav, the Bystander

Hi, Gustav,

Thanks for the long letter. The short answer is: STAY OUT OF IT.

YOU ARE NOT GOING TO CHANGE ANYTHING. THE MAN IS AN ADULTERER AND SHE IS A DING DONG. I HAVE FOUND IT IS BETTER TO STAY OUT OF FAMILY PROBLEMS WHEN NO ONE WILL CHANGE AND YOU WILL END UP BEING THE BAD GUY.

THE ROAD TO HELL IS PAVED WITH GOOD INTENTIONS.

Having said that, Let me ask you something, if this married man were sneaking around with YOUR sister and not your WIFE's sister, what would you do?

You got your answer, Bystander, you would nip it in the bud the minute you found out all the immorality going on under your in-laws's nose. Who knows how long this has been going on but it has got to stop. That's what a Gentleman does and that's why you are writing to me.

The faithless husband and his side chick are both at fault although I would say your Father-in-Law has something to do with it. First of all, the sister-in-law needs to get a real education so she can get a real job. So what that her old man is made of money, and gives his little girl an allowance so she does not need a 9 to 5? Even the Big 3 car companies are way past their hay day.

There's work to be done and people to work with. He needs to turn off the money tap. She is going to be no good as anyone's wife until the Dingaling Sister-in-law lives on her own and makes her own money and stands on her own two feet. At 20, she still has time to create value in society. And she needs a talking-to, maybe from your wife, to get therapy for her Daddy issues and stick to bachelors! In the Dating Dictionary, the Caprice who can live independently is the one worth marrying. Because she will make sure the little girls she has with you can work and think and are not vulnerable to two-bit married Shysters.

Speaking of Shysters, waiting for the Father-in-Law to kick the bucket is precisely what the Philandering Executive Assistant is doing. If he were really in an unhappy marriage where his wife doesn't understand him and he wanted a better life, the Shyster would talk to his wife about how to give them their freedom, pay her the alimony and child support like a man, and file the paperwork. Once he is AVAILABLE, then he can openly date and pursue anyone. He shows his hand by being underhanded - the sister-in-law's emotional affair with an older man is cloaked for public consumption ie her mother and father are duped into thinking it as an innocent crush.

Here is what you can do, turn a flashlight on. At the next family soiree or a meeting at the office, get your father-in-law and the Shyster and you together in a corner, a bit of privacy where ladies are present (if at the party). Take the initiative and open to the Old man, "Sir, I have to commend Shyster here, for his initiative to put to rest those silly affair rumours about him and your younger daughter. It is so important to preserve your daughter's reputation."

That lets the Shyster know the jig's up. And he can take his gigolo self elsewhere.

Remember, guys, a System man shines the light on Shysters, and leaves it to the main characters to sort it out.

CHAPTER NINE

9.My girlfriend has too much good baggage

Hello, Doc,

I am 25 and want to know about how to handle the baggage that comes with my Caprice. Really good baggage, this is an unusual take on baggage.

We've known each other since childhood as distant cousins but we really got to know each other as teenagers. My widowed grandmother lives close to her parents in London and I stay with her on breaks from boarding school, breaks from deployment, and my current job in the navy.

I think Caprice is the most wonderful thing and am gearing up to propose. We have been taking it slow, four years, and she is mad about me too. Her baggage however makes me hesitate. Her parents come from a very archaic form of Old Money and I'm talking about butlers, maids, riding stables, country houses, the whole shebang. She and her younger sister, 17, never even went to school. Top-notch

teachers would go to her house (take your pick of her country estates or London townhouse) to educate them. They do not ever have to work regular jobs. At 21, Caprice has always lived at home.

There's more. Her father, I get along with him, is grooming Caprice to take over from him as chairman of the business. They are word-dropping famous. Although it is not CEO or president with operational responsibilities , chairing a huge company might happen within the next few years as his health is not good. She would have to give up our future house wherever I am stationed and we would return to the London HQ and live in one of family homes. The nightmare scenario has me giving up my career in the navy to become the Chair's husband.

I did not go through years of training to become a landlubber of a househusband.

It's unnerving to me how her family is in each other's business. Plus, the household staff (butlers, personal dressers, footmen, etc) and corporate staff is overly influential into everything that happens in the family's private life. Is this normal? Maybe it is, I live on my salary, my own parents lead separate lives in different countries, and my four older sisters also live in yet another country which is definitely not normal.

Any advice, Doc, on a Caprice with too much of the good stuff?

Hank, The HandMan's Tale

Hello, Hank the HandMan,

You came to the only man in 6000 years who understands women. But my mission is to help guys so let's focus on you. Don't waste time parsing baggage. Baggage is baggage, what you have to do is decide if you can deal with the baggage of the specific Caprice.

First of all, let me thank you on behalf of all the members here for your service defending your country. At age 25, you deserve a happy home when not on deployment.

So, your Caprice and family are world famous, 'Lifestyles of the Rich and Famous' famous. You understand each other and have a lot in common, besides genetic material, I hope. Her Pops is preparing to pass on the figure headship of the family business to her. Something tells me that Pops is looking ahead, which is good. Obviously he likes you or he would have exiled you far away from his little princess. So far, so good.

Here is the first red flag, HandMan, she is 21. Sure she loves you NOW but in the Dating Dictionary, everyone under the age of 23 is a ding dong falling in and out of love every 5 minutes. What happens if you two marry now and she falls in love with one of Daddy's executive assistants? You would get the shaft and she would get your children, courtesy of the best lawyers her money can buy. Better wait til she out of that ding dong stage.

Of course her family approves of her marrying you soon; they probably planned it with Daddy's health situation in mind! Now, I am sorry his days are numbered but that is their problem, not yours. My job is to look out for you, not for you to be the sacrificial lamb for their benefit.

Red Flag #2 is a big one. Your Caprice is in her happy little solar system and it is a big unknown universe out there! Cocoon, she lives in a cottoncandy solar system cocoon with unicorns and pink little ponies! If she goes from country house to townhouse surrounded by staff and family, how does she meet real life? Oh, I forgot, you just said she still loves at home, never left home, and does not have a real job. There ain't no chance she and the littler princess accidentally meet ordinary people.

You, my friend, even though you are an outlier in their solar system, live among us peons, and since you don't have much money, you are one of us. Navy and Army and Air Force, good people all. Can you imagine how she reacts when her cushioned cotton candy world melts? You don't know and I don't know because she does not know. Do you want to be the husband who is the reason the princess leaves LaLa Land? We are not here to teach women how to function in the real world, we are here to meet women who already stand on her own two feet.

When Pops departs for heaven, you and the princess will return to live in her Planet of Plenty, that's red flag #3. How appealing to you is luxury living among the hive of spies, even if all the bills for the rest of your life are on her autopay? Hint: you wrote me.

It is part of life to fall in love with all sorts of Caprices but a System Guy only proposes to the flexible givers who are loyal, honest, and trustworthy and can stand on her own two feet.

Remember, guys: If you give up your livelihood in exchange for her megabucks paying for a lifetime of utility bills. it's not a trade-off you will live down.

CHAPTER TEN

10. Why the rush? Patience is the key to women

Hello, Doc Love,

A guy I grew up around advised me to email you, here's my situation. My big brother is a buzz-kill about my new girlfriend. He thinks we are moving too fast. But he doesn't get what's it like to be 32 and single. He met his wife at age 19 and they dated for 8 years before they married.

On the other hand, my last 2 serious girlfriends bailed because they didn't want to deal with the media (I come from a very high profile family - think 'Kennedy' times two). The two Caprices also complained I was too clingy and rushed too fast. And needed to get therapy because of my Mommy issues. (A year ago, I finally did it and am in a much better place.)

Two weeks ago, I finally found someone who is prepared to take me on. She's on a TV series, just finished its 6th season on cable. You wouldn't think she's older than me by 4 years, she's in real good shape and looks great. She has no baggage as she ended a ten-year relationship a couple years ago - they had been married the last year-and-a-half years. With her charity work, she is not shy in advocating for others in front of the camera. I do charity work too.

Friends had set us up on a blind date on a Friday, and it was like meeting my dream. I texted her right after and for the past week, we've been in constant contact.

In another three weeks, she has to cross the Atlantic to report to set to shoot another season, and I have been getting in all the dates I can. The London summer is the best!

I am well-fixed for money and don't have to work so I plan to whisk her away to Africa this weekend for a week. But my older married brother tells me to slow down. He's wrong to rain on my parade, and I got so mad that I just turned around and left.

I always say, Carpe diem, Seize the day. Mom had died in a car accident when I was 12, and since then I don't waste time.

If you know, you just know. She's so incredible.

How can I convince my brother 2 tickets to Africa is the best sign of commitment to my new relationship?

Ivo, I Found The One

<u>Hello, Ivo I Found,</u>

You know what you need to find? Your American Express Blue card to order The Dating Dictionary and phone coaching with DocLove. After two women with their heads screwed on went and dumped you, you headed their good advice on therapy. And now your buddy has referred you to me, Doc Love. You got a good friend in him. He could have picked up the phone to TMZ and made a killing with an exclusive about KennedyTimesTwo and the Cable TV Actress, instead, he shows his loyalty by sending you to the best, that's me, Doc Love. You are obviously used to paying for the best, grasshopper.

First of all, your letter was all about YOU and your high Interest Level in this Beautiful Woman. Like all guys who have not mastered The Dating Dictionary, the high Interest Level you have in her doesn't count. What she thinks and feels about you do count.

Like all men who go start salivating at a stunning Caprice, you give this Beautiful Woman who is also an Actress too much credit. A TV actress has to keep in shape and be comfortable in front of the camera - that comes with the territory. If she were not happy to show her teeth to an TV audience, she would be replaced by another pretty actress who knows her lines and loves the lens and applause. As my cousin Lucky Luke Love from Hollywood, California says, "I'm spoiled for choice!"

You talk about 'if you know, you just know.' Well, what do you know after two weeks of dating? Nothing. And your condensed dating counts for nothing. And only after 10 dates stretched over 3 months is what really counts, because anyone can fake it for 5 days or 30 days, but not in the long run. You cannot get to know someone in a shorter period of time, so the same applies to you from the perspective of this beautiful Actress. What she does know after 2 weeks that you don't have the self-control to stay off the cell phone, can flash the cash, and have plenty of leisure time penciled into your calendar.

And she knows that she is the only one you are dating. You should never be exclusive with someone you hardly know, Boy, you have surrendered to her the power of the Rejection Card!

You simply don't have enough information or time in to decide if she is The One. Unlike laundry detergent, you cannot get to know her Integrity and her Scars & Baggage any better by concentrating 10 dates into one week. How do I know your MO? The two women who dumped you say you rush and cling. And you just wrote that you have been texting and talking and going out with this latest. You haven't learnt much from their friendly feedback!

There is a huge difference between wasting time and giving it time. In your horse lessons, have you heard about 'rushing the fences'? That's what happens when you don't give time for her Interest Level to rise. Seeing time as an ALLY instead of an enemy converts it into Challenge. And Challenge is kryptonite to women.

How can you convince your brother? How about you keep your private life to yourself and stop talking about the women you date to all your buddies? Oversharing comes across as lacking confidence, and Confidence is what appeals to a good woman and keeps a good woman in love with you. Here is what works: you go out with a variety of women, decide who are the good ones, date the ladies where there is mutual liking, and give two years to the Flexible Giver with honesty, loyalty, and trust. You don't need to tell anyone a dang thing. Your brother will then take you aside and say, "We all think she's great, you have to pop the question."

Remember, guys: When everyone thinks you are rushing in with your wallet, you probably are.

CHAPTER ELEVEN

11. A brother-in-law with convictions...

Hello, Doc,

I have been following you online and read some of your articles. You support us men from the dating to the marrying. I am in a bit of a quandary and would like to ask your help in keeping my household happy. My sister and her husband are causing problems in my marriage.

Caprice and I are happily married with two young daughters. My job in the family business is going well as I am groomed to take over from my father. My wife is as committed to the business as well, working part time, as do my sisters to a lesser extent. At important company functions, my two sisters and their husbands just show up to press the flesh.

My folks worked hard and brought us up to live the good life. The husband of my younger sister, an ex-minor league sports pro, has always felt he lacked what it takes to give her the lifestyle she has grown accustomed to. He's right about that and that's why he is now in trouble with the law.

It is a bit cliché to say he always acts like a big shot. When the family gets together, he is always bragging about a deal for his company. It turns out he and his partner are accused of inflating contracts with the state government. He also used his company's coffers like a personal piggy bank – and the IRA doesn't like that.

As my sister is on the books as a company director, she doesn't come out looking good either. Whether she is pretending not to know about the fraud or doesn't care about the fraud, she is not lying about leaving the mundane paperwork up to him. She always a bit of an ostrich when it comes to how money is earned. They are pleading innocent to charges of embezzlement, defrauding the government, and probably littering.

The family company is fending off collateral damage from my brother-in-law and sister's legal issues. My wife says we should not be in contact with them at all while it gets before the courts. My mother says we should be publicly united as a family on this. Myself, I am pretty steamed that they ran a house-of-cards that could potentially take us all down.

So, Doc, what should I do?

Liam, Living with family convictions

Hello, Liam,

Women don't lie and I have interviewed over 10,000 of them. You bet I know the keys to making them happy. Because they tell me and I listen and I share. That's the kind of guy I am. In my columns, I give you just the gist of what I have spent forty years putting together. To get deeper and to keep your marriage happy, you need to join the other Spartans out there and buy The Dating Dictionary.

You found a good one in Caprice, who seems a good wife to you and a good mother to those little girls, and making a meaningful contribution to the family business. Your brothers-in-law put on a good show to the public but maybe that is all they are capable to doing.

A little trouble in paradise shows up when your sister marries Al Bundy. Brother-in-law is now in trouble with the law with his big-shot-itis. And your sister is the dingdong, "As long as the credit card bills are paid, honey, I don't want to know the details."

The long arm of the law and the bad publicity can affect your happy home. Here's how I know you married a good girl: She is loyal to you. Other women would have packed their bags and flown the coop but Caprice is staying with you. As my cousin Fast Eddie Love from East LA says, "When there's smoke, the party girl doesn't want it near her hair."

Your Caprice is staying because Her Interest Level in you must be through the roof. You must be doing something right.

As a Gentleman of the System, you owe it to her to be the man she fell in love with. The guy who showed her Confidence, Self-Control, and Challenge. In this situation, you have to show her your Confidence in handling the bad press and the stinking pile of dog poop your sister and brother-in-law have left in their wake. The Spartans of the System do not condone wrongdoing nor do we support wrongdoers. What kind of example does that set for your daughters to be seen in public wining and dining with the Wall Street types who got us into this mess? In this case,

Mom is wrong. The System guy is united in the cause for justice.

Remember, guys, your main responsibilities as a Gentlemen are to your wife and children. The other adults in your life have to take care of their own mess.

CHAPTER TWELVE:

12. My fiancée's family aren't invited to our Big Fat Wedding... so they've gone nuts

Hello, Doc,

I am not a snob but my fiancee's family think I am just because they are not invited to our wedding. It was not my idea to leave them off the guest list as I think 'the more, the merrier'. My side has the cash to host two times as many as the cathedral holds and we can always bring in more caterers and pitch another tent for the reception.

It was my Caprice who does not want them there. She has had an arm's-length relationship with her mother and half-siblings from the second marriage for a long time. I go along with Whatever makes her happy.

They think it's my idea since we did not attend her mother's annual Thanksgiving do prior to our

engagement. In fact I have never met them as Caprice did not want to do the turkey thing. You Americans have very peculiar holidays. They blame me but it was her call not to go. I have to admit to being protective of her from what she calls their toxicity.

I also defend her to my own people. I know you don't approve of PDA, Doc, but I feel it is natural to not hold back on how much we are in love. As she hugs everyone, it is so easy to let myself go. That kind of thing is really not done in my more conservative country and people have called her on it. I am in her corner on her natural exuberance to my tribe and she's new to her soon-to-be home.

About the non-invite - her family just won't let it it go and they blame me and my family for being snobs. Now they are blowing this thing up on social media about the 'snub'. I guess it should not have surprised us as she has always had a conflicted relationship with her step and half brothers and sisters. Some of them she has given the silent treatment for years so I think it take a lot of nerve to expect an invite to a classy high society wedding.

It's not that they get drunk or can't behave in church but she finds her father's entire family toxic. Hey, it's her wedding too and if they aren't invited, they should just act like adults.

She is in tears about the social media storm and I am beside myself on what to do to make her feel better. What do you suggest, Doc?

Karl, No-Room for Drama

<u>Hello, Karl</u>,

This is what happens when you pop the question: wedding drama.

About your fiancee's family feeling snubbed; well, because they were! Regardless of the reason like limited budget or snobbery or bride holding a grudge, any time family members don't get an invitation to a happy event, they feel rejected. In the Dating Dictionary, I explain that rejection is a feeling people don't like to feel. Most people feel really strongly about being on the other end of the rejection card. But as my cousin Fast Eddy Love from East LA says, "If you don't invite me to a party, I got better replacements lined up. But not everybody's like me!"

The classy thing to do, high-society wedding or not, is invite everyone in the family to the wedding. Because weddings are where you bring people together; they are not the place to settle scores.

I have seen couple avoid inconvenient guests by eloping. There's a reason people tie the knot at five-star resorts all the way in the Caribbean - when you choose destination weddings that most invitees can't afford, they self-select out. As my cousin Fast Eddy Love from East LA say, "They do your dirty work for you!"

On the other hand, just because you invite everybody doesn't mean you intend to lose money on hosting this event. You can pick and choose who gets to eat at your expense, did you not read your Emily Post? Invite everyone to the wedding but invite only the A-listers to the seated meal. Take a tip from the British party family – Pippa Middleton had to invite drunk Uncle Gary to the wedding but he was going nowhere near the wedding supper. If you really want to save money, two words: cash bar.

You can let Mother Nature pick the venue. Here in Southern California, life's a beach, and you can get great shots for free at a public beach.

Here's what you could do – grin and bear it. your fiancée phones each one up, lies through her pearly-white teeth that the US Postal Service messed it up, and FedEx invitations to the church ceremony, along with the Bergdorf Goodman gift registry.

If they can't fork out the plane fare and hotel rooms and the Bergdorf and Tiffany gift registry , que sera sera. We will send you a thank-you note for that $200 gift.

If they do show up, you can seat them in social Siberia. Or put her whacky relatives with your whacky relatives (admit it, you have them too!) and budget extra security to monitor that table so she doesn't have to. Or better yet, put them around people who aren't on social media. Like I tell you guys, stay off Facebook and Twitter.

You weren't there when she was growing up so you have no idea what's what. However, this raises a Red Flag. If she can give her own family the 'silent treatment', that kind of manipulative behaviour can turn on your people. Looking at her pattern, what makes you think that she won't also turn against your own family?

Or you, for that matter? Worse would be if you two have a kid and she used the baby as leverage against you. And you would let her, to keep her. Because you are not a challenge, giving her everything, in your own words, to keep her happy.

Remember, guys, money can't buy you class but it can pay for a classy wedding.

CHAPTER THIRTEEN

13. My wife says I need a purpose...

Hello, Doc Love,

Greetings to you in sunny southern California from wintry Europe. I am writing to you in hopes you can assist me with a marital issue. My wife does not like our life while I am perfectly happy with it. This is affecting our 3 year old while his 11 month old brother might feel the tension too.

I come from an old family which has had money and influence for generations. We have houses in five cities in Europe and I myself live in a country estate when not in a town house in our country's cosmopolitan capital. Every month, I derive a handsome income from family trusts so there is no need for me to work full time. I put on a few appearances monthly and that keeps everyone in the stakeholder circle happy.

We met when I was in her country doing a 9-month work internship in one of the world's global centres of

finance. She was ambitious, well-travelled junior executive , and easy on the eyes and doesn't look 4 years my senior, and it was a whirlwind courtship. I invited her to my country after my work term ended and she accepted my proposal.

Looking back, we did not know each other very well. She chaffes as country living and my laid-back approach to life. Every chance she gets, she is at the townhouse. Having learnt our languuage, all sorts of charities want her on board. She wants me to be more proactive and business-active. I have no interest in an executive role.

My brother is next in line and I am glad to be born #2. Am out of the spotlight and I can lead life pretty much how I want. On a working farm, Mother Nature determines what is on tap. When it rains, you just do something else inside the stables or the barn. That's just the way it is.

My wife just chomps on the bit and stomps around the castle that she can't stand. She is spending more and more time away and the boys hardly miss her because of the good nannies. I am tired of her saying I stifled her future. Sure she was an executive but give me a break, my family's lifestyle is something she would never have gotten no matter how much she worked. In the old parlance, 'she married well' but unlike the GoldDiggers you mentioned in the Dating Dictionary, she doesn't seem to appreciate it.

I like my life the way things are, ,especially when she is out. Because that way, she is not nagging at me to be someone I am not.

So, Doc, what should I do?

Signed, OldMacDonald The FarmGuy

<u>Hello, Old MacDonald,</u>

I have to say, OldMacDonald, that you are a living breathing example of a man who rushed into marriage. And look at what that got you - a wife who doesn't appreciate that her man's home is his castle. Cause I bet that is what your country home really is, an honest-to-goodness castle.

You have the attitude of gratitude, I bet you get along with your folks and in-laws because of your maturity. You are a farm boy and make no apologies for it.

A few appearances in the big city every month and in return, they leave you be in the countryside. This arrangement makes you happy but infuriates her. If you had dated for 2 years and not rushed into marriage, you would have found out that she prefers it the other way around: she's a little bit country, she's a lot more spotlight in the city!

Now she's acting on it. As my cousin General Love puts it, "Sounds like she is establishing a beach head." She is setting up a life in the city - without you! And why not? You are happier when she is out and not nagging you.

What you should do is lawyer up. When a wife starts hitting the bright lights, she has less than 49%

percent Interest Level in you and it is just a matter of time before she finds a replacement for you. Those divorce papers are going to get filed sooner or later so why not beat her to the punch?

On your next Match.com profile, write 'must love the country, harvesting, and farm animals.'

Remember, guys, if you're happy and you know it, then don't change.

Chapter Fourteen:

14. She's wife material but not C-Suite wife material

Hello, Doc Love,

I am 38 years young, grateful loyal Spartan of the System for five years, which has brought me close to the pinnacle of my career. With the System changing my life, I studied hard, started from the ground floor, took as many postings internationally aa possible, and worked my way up the corporate ladder. That is why I got the interim CEO position, I out competed the landlubber lazy-assed cousins in the family business. Just a few months ago, I relocated back to our European HQ. Doc, things are looking sweet from the C-Suite.

I can now call the shots, and have delegated a lot of the unnecessary travel. This is because I am ready to settle down and start a family and I can commit to being a good husband and father. I can even foresee public service at some point.

You know about the Law of Attraction, I am dating some very nice women and have filtered in those who are 'wife material'. But here's my dilemmma, Doc, one Caprice I really like is wife material but she is not an obvious 'C-suite wife material'.

In the two months since we met, she is very nice and easy on the eyes and we share many of the same interests, mostly country pursuits and animals. She knows about my journey to the top and wants to adapt to my lifestyle. Just a week ago, her new passport arrived in the mail, that's how proactive she is.

So I slowly introduced her to colleagues and family but Caprice almost faints in a setting of more than 5 strangers. She is almost mute, looks down at the floor, and is passive. If it weren't for my explaining about her shyness, people would think she is rude and abrupt. Invariably, within half an hour, Caprice makes for the door and I go with her. After all, I am a Gentleman.

So, Doc, what else should I do? I genuinely think she is special but I wonder what I can do as I am heading for the C-suite.

Nick, My Next Office is the CornerOffice

Hello, Nick,

Always good to read a You Changed My Life letter, Jeff and I are here to help men become Gentlemen. The System helps men become productive members of society, that's my public service.

Some men think they are on the clock when it comes to marriage but System guys don't rush it. As my cousin Reverend Love says, "To every thing, there is a season. You plant, you fertilize, you harvest."

Speaking of farm language, Caprice knows all about gardening, which is a sign she is not a shopaholic. Kudos for you to be attracted to grounded salt-of-the-earth women. You like her, even I like her, and I haven't even met her!

Now, I am all for liking and you like her now but for how much longer? Every time you do something that is part of your executive job, her reaction raises Red Flags. Then you have to step in to explain her conduct.

Guy, she is not able to stand on her own two feet in a social function! You know that social functions are a part of your climb to the top. Networking is where things happen. It is essential and she knows that but she can't help it.

I get it that she can't help it but the point you are missing is she can't help you. Remember what I say, if she likes you, she helps you? How helpful is bolting for the exit door so you can chase after her like a nanny? Cutting short an appearance means you don't do your job properly. How long do you think the bosses will put up with a guy who is distracted from his job? Those lazy cousins of yours may be silent sharks just waiting for you to slip up and then boom, you are on an elevator ride down to a posting in Alaska.

Her hang ups are making her less appealing. In this case, it is the guy's Interest Level that is falling, a few points here, a few points there. Resentment does that to anybody and then before you know it, your Interest Level falls below 49%. We all know what that means.

She is who she is. She ain't gonna change and she is going to resent you for putting her in situations she is uncomfortable in. (Ever seen the Sissi movies or heard of the story of Empress Elisabeth of Austria?) If you plan to move to the country side and take up being a gentleman farmer, she's tailor made for that. But don't fool yourself that you can give up your high-powered executive lifestyle for her. Because you deep down do not want to. Why should you? You invested all this time and filled your passport. She just got a passport. See what I mean? You are in your element and she is out of hers. Reality never lies, my friend.

The beauty is, because you did not rush in like all the other turkeys, you didn't ask her to be the girlfriend, and now you won't. The System saves you as you hadn't even gotten past 3 months. And now you know.

What you should do is let her go. As a Gentleman, call her up and go to her place. Tell her that you crossed paths with an ex at meeting or conference, that you two reconnected (women respect seniority!), and have decided to give it a go. That lets her down as best as you can. In this case, honesty (your passivity has lowered my Interest Level to 49%) is not the best policy. We aren't here to hurt women, we are here to get rid of women as nicely as possible.

Then go get other phone numbers.

Remember, guys, It does not matter how many interests you have in common, if you don't share a future, that's the entire truth. When the truth shows up at your door step, as I said before, Believe It Now. The smart money says Next!

###

The System For Her Series

Adapting the wisdom of DocLove with examples from the over 130 Harlequin/Mills & Boon books by Betty Neels, Janice Seto's The System for Her series provides clear insight into the mysterious behaviour of women and men in pursuit of their Happily Ever After.

Part 1: Doc Love Lessons in Betty Neels Books

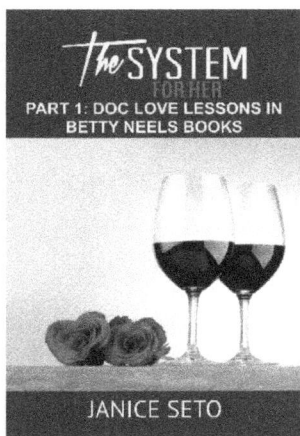

The System for Her, Part 1: Doc Love Lessons from Betty Neels books shows how extensive research by Doc Love (www.doclove.com) into successful relationships takes shape in the gentlemen and the ladies in the Harlequin/Mills & Boon books by Mrs. Neels - and these translate into timeless lessons for today's modern reader.

https://www.amazon.com/System-Her-Part-Lessons-Betty/dp/1926935225/

Part 2: Doc Love Lessons in Betty Neels Heroes

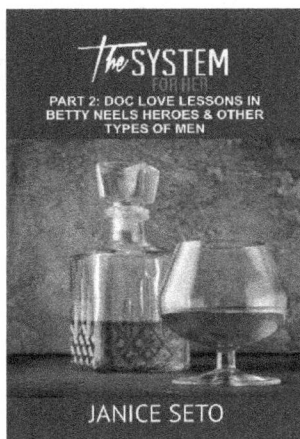

In this second book on relationships inspired by Doc Love, this time author Janice Seto puts the men in Betty Neels romances under the microscope. The System for Women, Part 2: Doc Love Lessons in Betty Neels Heroes introduces you to the ideal hero, the Gentleman and his hangers-on that include the Macho Boy, the Teddy Bear, the Wimpus Americanus.

https://www.amazon.com/System-Her-Part-Lessons-Heroes-ebook/dp/B071WQDJC6

Part 3: Doc Love Lessons in Betty Neels Heroines

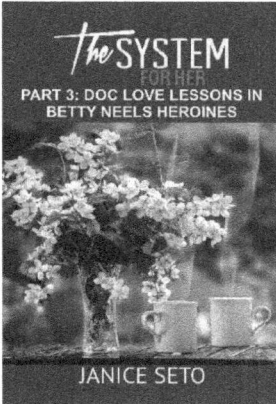

In this third book on relationships inspired by DocLove, Janice Seto uncovers key nuggets of female happiness. *The System for Women, Part 3: Doc Love Lessons in Betty Neels Heroines*, keeps it simple. Bid good-bye to Blockers, Veronicas, and embrace your timesaving Reality Factors and The Bottom Line.

https://www.amazon.com/gp/product/B07FK635TB

Part 4: Doc Love Lessons in Betty Neels Happily Ever After

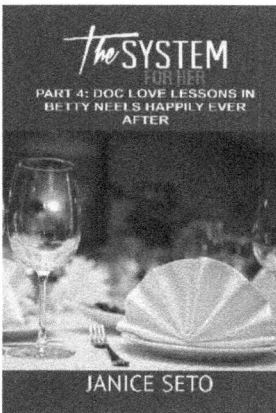

In this fourth book on relationships inspired by DocLove, Janice Seto looks past 'I do'. The System for Women, Part 4: Doc Love Lessons in Betty Neels Happily Ever After lays out Doc Love's Maintenance Program for keeping Ms Right in love. The author also reveals the three Black Swans of a hell-on-earth relationship. This book is a must for the couple who truly wants to live Happily Ever After.

https://www.amazon.com/gp/product/B07FK635TB

Part 5: Doc Love Lessons in Pride and Prejudice

ABOUT THE AUTHOR

Janice Seto writes non-fiction and commentary including articles for The Bridge, the publication of The Malaysia-Canada Business Council. Her most recent books are available in ebook and print format: *Standing Out in The Background – A Guide to Extra Work in Toronto's Film & TV Industry*, *Segovia Restaurant – Espana in Toronto by Ino*, *Johnny's Place - The Coronation Restaurant in Bowmanville*, and *Johnny Seto's Bowmanville – An Enneagram Perspective*. *Bowmanville's Octagon House – From Church and Faith and Tait to Irwin & Seto* also went all the way to #1.

The System for Her is her first book series on relationships, based on the hilarious but insightful work of Doc Love http://www.doclove.com/ referencing the books of Betty Neels. Betty Neels is the modern Jane Austen – give it a few more years, and the world will be convinced, not just the ladies of The Uncrushable Jersey Dress blog, http://everyneelsthing.blogspot.com/

Works in progress by Janice Seto include a travel guide series designed for the JKC tourist (Japanese, Korean, Chinese). When you travel, you need tourist information and recommendations that are pertinent to you. JKC Travel Guides help you get the most of your vacation. JKC's Ireland and JKC's Argentina are available in ebook format at https://www.amazon.com/gp/product/B07MXV545Y https://www.amazon.com/gp/product/B07RSV4K8B

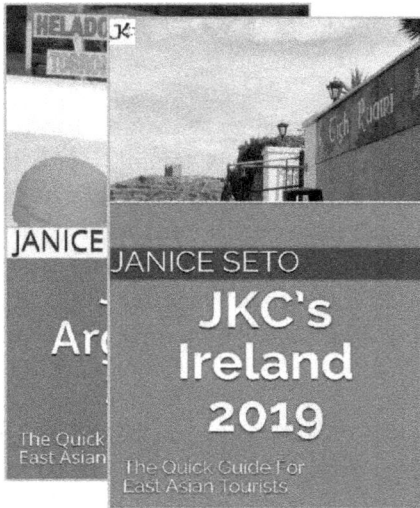

The first book in the *Royalty Meets Enneagram* series on the Enneagram personality typology, *Royalty Meets Enneagram: Understanding Personality Style 7: Meghan Markle, Sarah Ferguson, Princess Tessy*, was published in time for the 2018 royal wedding.
https://www.amazon.com/gp/product/1926935365

Janice gets her laughs via the Doc Love podcast and weekly radio show, accessible to members of the DocLoveClub http://www.doclove.com/ . Newcomers welcome!

http://janiceseto.wixsite.com/words/blog
http://janiceseto.wix.com/words
www.janiceseto.com